DISCARDED

Date: 4/3/12

J BIO KANE
Stone, Adam.
Kane /

KANE

BY ADAM STONE

Are you ready to take it to the extreme?
Torque books thrust you into the action-packed world
of sports, vehicles, mystery, and adventure. These books
may include dirt, smoke, fire, and dangerous stunts.
WARNING : read at your own risk.

Library of Congress Cataloging-in-Publication Data

Stone, Adam.
Kane / by Adam Stone.
    p. cm. -- (Torque: pro wrestling champions)
Includes bibliographical references and index.
Summary: "Engaging images accompany information about Kane. The combination of high-interest
subject matter and light text is intended for students in grades 3 through 7"--Provided by publisher.
ISBN 978-1-60014-637-4 (hardcover : alk. paper)
1. Jacobs, Glenn T., 1967--- Juvenile literature. 2. Wrestlers--United States--Biography--Juvenile
literature. I. Title. II. Series.

GV1196.J335S76 2011
796.812092--dc22
[B]   2011008660

This edition first published in 2012 by Bellwether Media, Inc.

CONTENTS

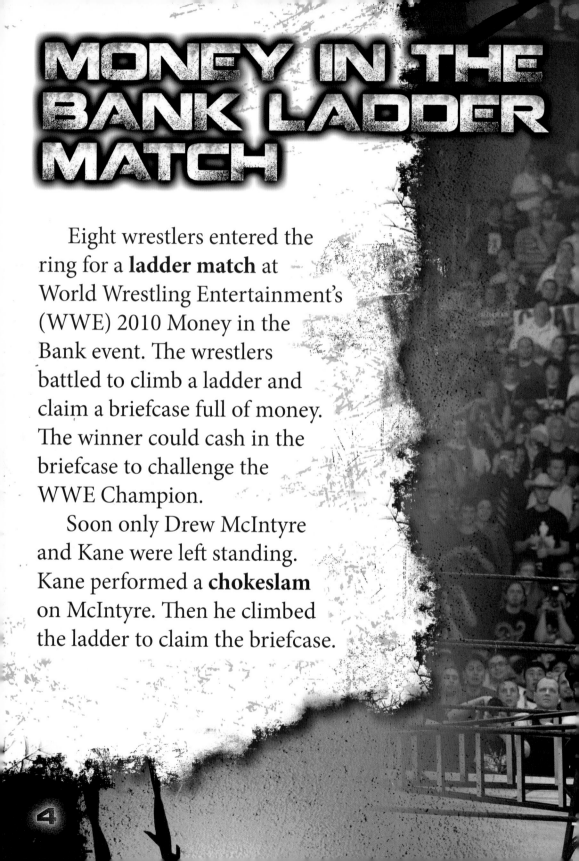

MONEY IN THE BANK LADDER MATCH

Eight wrestlers entered the ring for a **ladder match** at World Wrestling Entertainment's (WWE) 2010 Money in the Bank event. The wrestlers battled to climb a ladder and claim a briefcase full of money. The winner could cash in the briefcase to challenge the WWE Champion.

Soon only Drew McIntyre and Kane were left standing. Kane performed a **chokeslam** on McIntyre. Then he climbed the ladder to claim the briefcase.

4

5

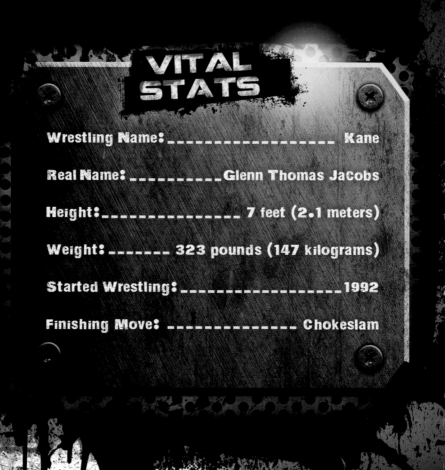

Later that night, Rey Mysterio won his World Heavyweight Championship match against Jack Swagger. When the match ended, Kane came out with his briefcase. He traded it for the chance to wrestle Mysterio and win the WWE Championship belt.

REY MYSTERIO

Mysterio was tired from his match. Kane easily overpowered him and chokeslammed him into the mat. Then he performed a brutal **Tombstone Piledriver.** Mysterio was knocked out. Kane covered him for the pin and became the new WWE Champion.

WHO IS KANE?

QUICK HIT!
One of Kane's nicknames is the "Big Red Monster." He got this name because of his size and strength.

Kane's real name is Glenn Thomas Jacobs. He was born on April 26, 1967 in Madrid, Spain. His parents were stationed there for the United States Air Force. Jacobs grew up near St. Louis, Missouri. His size and strength made him a good athlete. He played basketball and football in high school.

After high school, Jacobs got a **scholarship** to play basketball for Truman State University in Kirksville, Missouri. He studied hard and earned a degree in English. After college, Jacobs worked in a group home for adults with developmental disabilities. One of his co-workers was trying to become a wrestler. Jacobs decided to train with him.

QUICK HIT!

Jacobs holds a Truman State basketball record for field goals. In one season, he made 6 out of every 10 field goals he attempted.

Jacobs was 25 years old when he wrestled in his first match. He eventually quit his job to go to a wrestling school in Florida. After that he wrestled in small leagues across the United States. He wrestled as Doomsday.

BECOMING A CHAMPION

In 1995, WWE signed Jacobs to a contract. Jacobs wrestled as Dr. Isaac Yankem and later as Fake Diesel. His name changed to Kane in 1997. Kane was a **heel** and was called "half-man, half-monster." He wore a mask and did not speak.

QUICK HIT!

In 2003, Kane took off his mask for the first time. He has wrestled without it ever since.

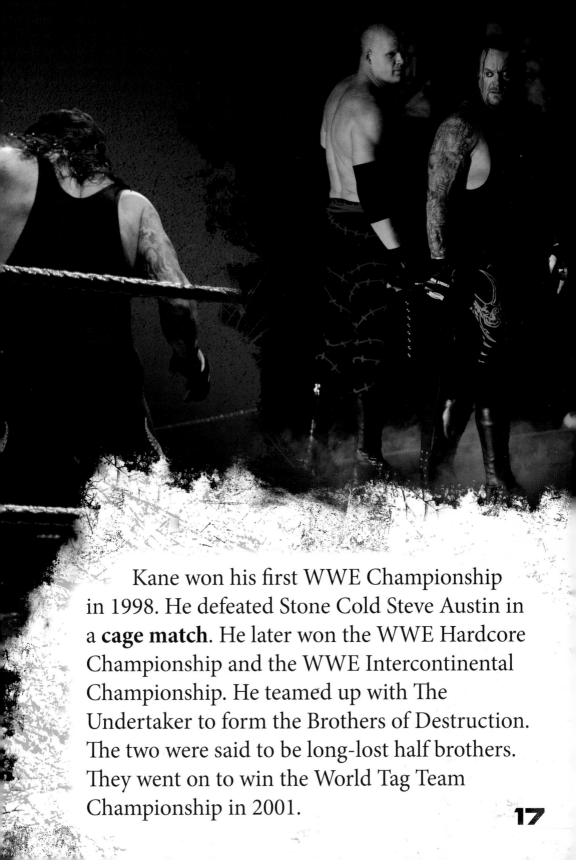

Kane won his first WWE Championship in 1998. He defeated Stone Cold Steve Austin in a **cage match**. He later won the WWE Hardcore Championship and the WWE Intercontinental Championship. He teamed up with The Undertaker to form the Brothers of Destruction. The two were said to be long-lost half brothers. They went on to win the World Tag Team Championship in 2001.

17

Kane is one of the biggest and most powerful wrestlers in WWE. He has several **signature moves**. One is the powerslam. He lifts his opponent over his shoulder. Then he slams him down to the mat and lands on top of him. Another is the clothesline. Kane charges at his opponent and drives his arm into the wrestler's neck.

QUICK HIT!

Kane has also appeared in movies. He had roles in *See No Evil* and *MacGruber*.

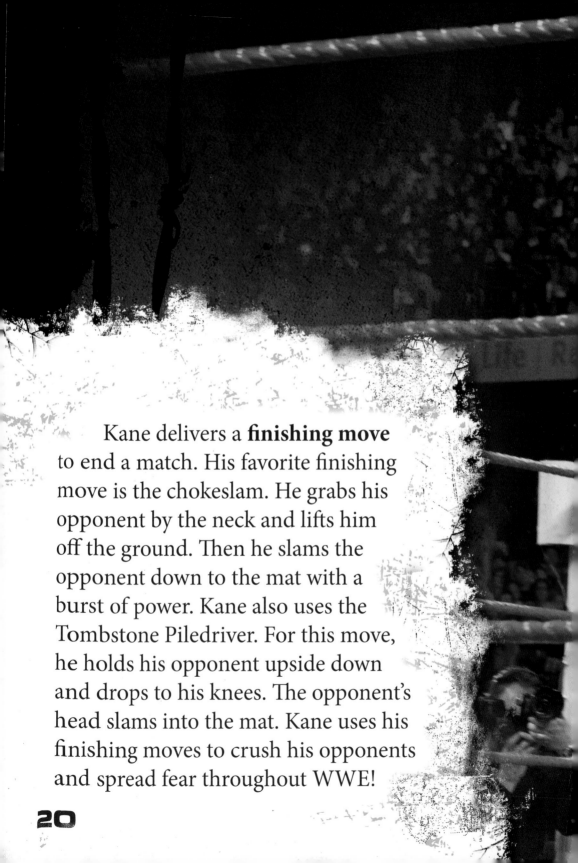

Kane delivers a **finishing move** to end a match. His favorite finishing move is the chokeslam. He grabs his opponent by the neck and lifts him off the ground. Then he slams the opponent down to the mat with a burst of power. Kane also uses the Tombstone Piledriver. For this move, he holds his opponent upside down and drops to his knees. The opponent's head slams into the mat. Kane uses his finishing moves to crush his opponents and spread fear throughout WWE!

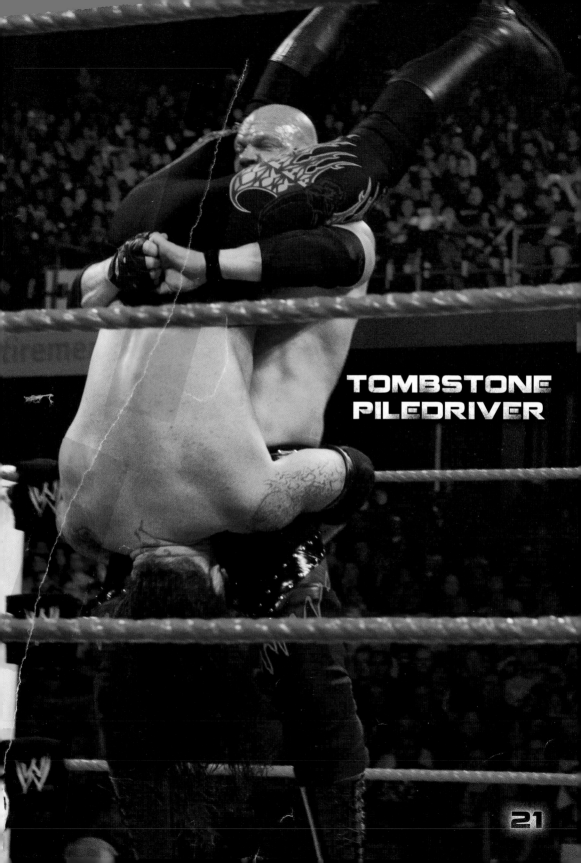

TOMBSTONE PILEDRIVER

GLOSSARY

cage match—a match in which wrestlers are locked inside a cage; no one can leave the cage until the match is over.

chokeslam—Kane's finishing move; he picks up a wrestler by the neck and slams him down to the mat.

finishing move—a wrestling move meant to finish off an opponent so that he can be pinned

heel—a wrestler seen by fans as a villain

ladder match—a wrestling match in which a ladder is placed in the middle of the ring; the first wrestler to reach the object at the top wins the match.

scholarship—money given to a student to pay for school

signature moves—moves that a wrestler is famous for performing

Tombstone Piledriver—a move in which a wrestler picks up his opponent, holds him upside down between his knees, and drops him headfirst onto the mat; Kane sometimes uses the Tombstone Piledriver as a finishing move.

TO LEARN MORE

AT THE LIBRARY

Black, Jake. *The Ultimate Guide to WWE*. New York, N.Y.: Grosset & Dunlap, 2010.

Kaelberer, Angie Peterson. *Cool Pro Wrestling Facts*. Mankato, Minn.: Capstone Press, 2011.

Stone, Adam. *The Undertaker*. Minneapolis, Minn.: Bellwether Media, 2012.

ON THE WEB

Learning more about Kane is as easy as 1, 2, 3.

1. Go to www.factsurfer.com.

2. Enter "Kane" into the search box.

3. Click the "Surf" button and you will see a list of related Web sites.

With factsurfer.com, finding more information is just a click away.

INDEX